DENTIST'S TOOLS

MARY ELIZABETH SALZMANN

Consulting Editor, Diane Craig, M.A./Reading Specialist

A Division of ABDO

ABDO
Publishing Company

visit us at www.abdopublishing.com

Published by ABDO Publishing Company, a division of ABDO,
P.O. Box 398166, Minneapolis, Minnesota 55439. Copyright © 2011
by Abdo Consulting Group, Inc. International copyrights reserved in
all countries. No part of this book may be reproduced in any form
without written permission from the publisher. Super SandCastle™
is a trademark and logo of ABDO Publishing Company.

Printed in the United States of America,
North Mankato, Minnesota
092010
012011

Editor: Liz Salzmann
Content Developer: Nancy Tuminelly
Photo Credits: Shutterstock
Special thanks to Dawn Bringelson, Midwest Archeological Center
and Kate Erickson, Anthropological Studies Center, Sonoma State
University.

Library of Congress Cataloging-in-Publication Data

Salzmann, Mary Elizabeth, 1968-
  Dentist's tools / Mary Elizabeth Salzmann.
    p. cm. -- (Professional tools)
  ISBN 978-1-61613-578-2
  1. Dentistry--Juvenile literature. 2. Children--Preparation for
dental care--Juvenile literature. I. Title.
  RK63.S25 2011
  617.6--dc22
                            2010018607

Super SandCastle™ books are created by a team of professional
educators, reading specialists, and content developers around
five essential components—phonemic awareness, phonics,
vocabulary, text comprehension, and fluency—to assist young
readers as they develop reading skills and strategies and
increase their general knowledge. All books are written,
reviewed, and leveled for guided reading, early reading
intervention, and Accelerated Reader® programs for use in
shared, guided, and independent reading and writing activities to
support a balanced approach to literacy instruction.

CONTENTS

GOING TO THE DENTIST

WHAT DOES A DENTIST DO?

Dentists keep people's teeth strong and healthy. People go to the dentist for regular **checkups**. The dentist cleans their teeth. Dentists also teach people how to take better care of their teeth.

WHY DO DENTISTS NEED TOOLS?

Some dentist's tools are used to check whether your teeth are healthy. Other tools are used to clean your teeth and remove **cavities**.

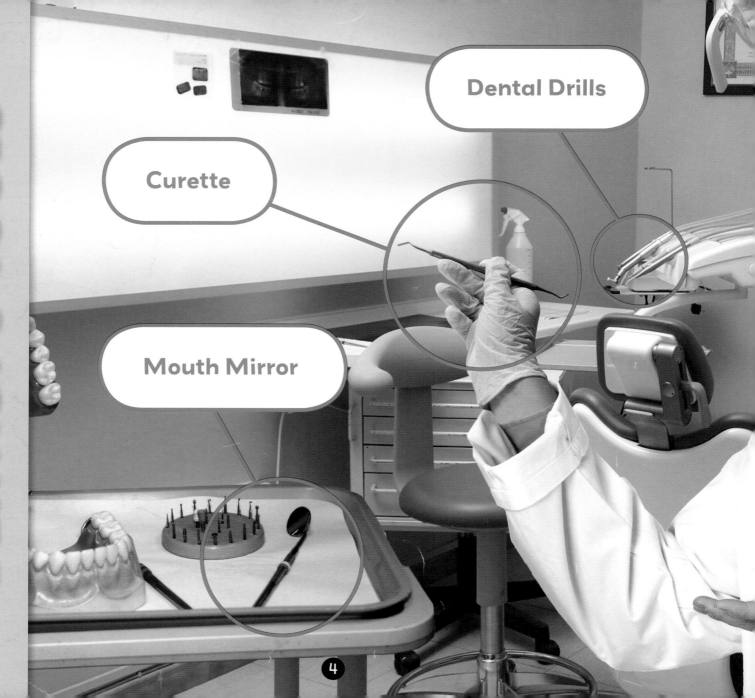

DENTIST'S TOOLS

Dental Drills

Curette

Mouth Mirror

X-ray Machine

MOUTH MIRROR

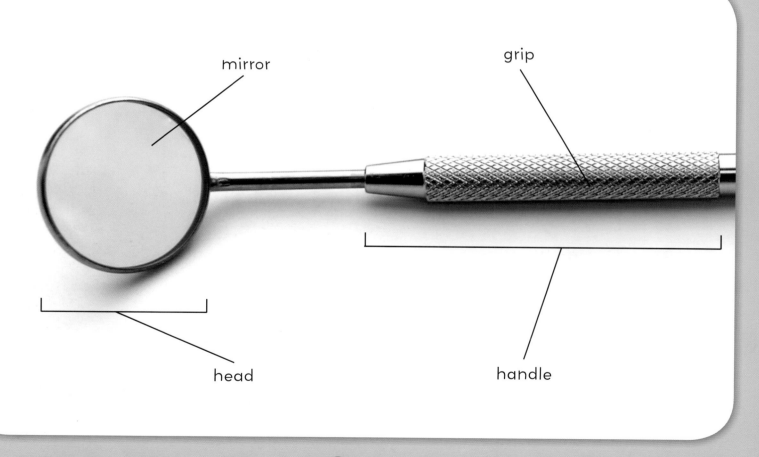

mirror

grip

head

handle

A mouth mirror helps the dentist see the teeth better.

Molars and the backs of the teeth are hard to see. The dentist puts the head of the mirror into the mouth. The dentist moves it around to see all of the teeth.

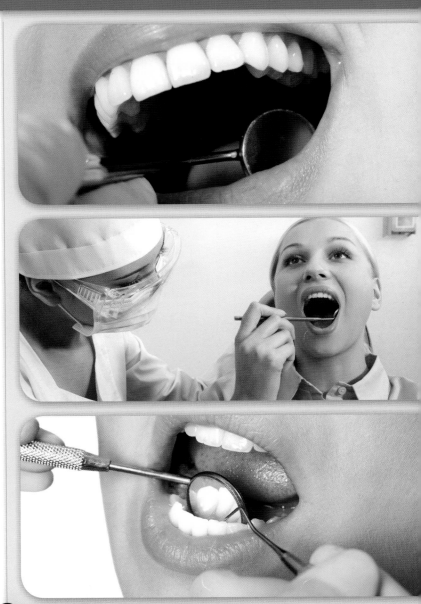

The dentist checks Amanda's teeth for **cavities**.
She is using a mouth mirror.

Jonas is getting a **checkup**. The dentist uses a mouth mirror to look at his teeth.

CURETTE

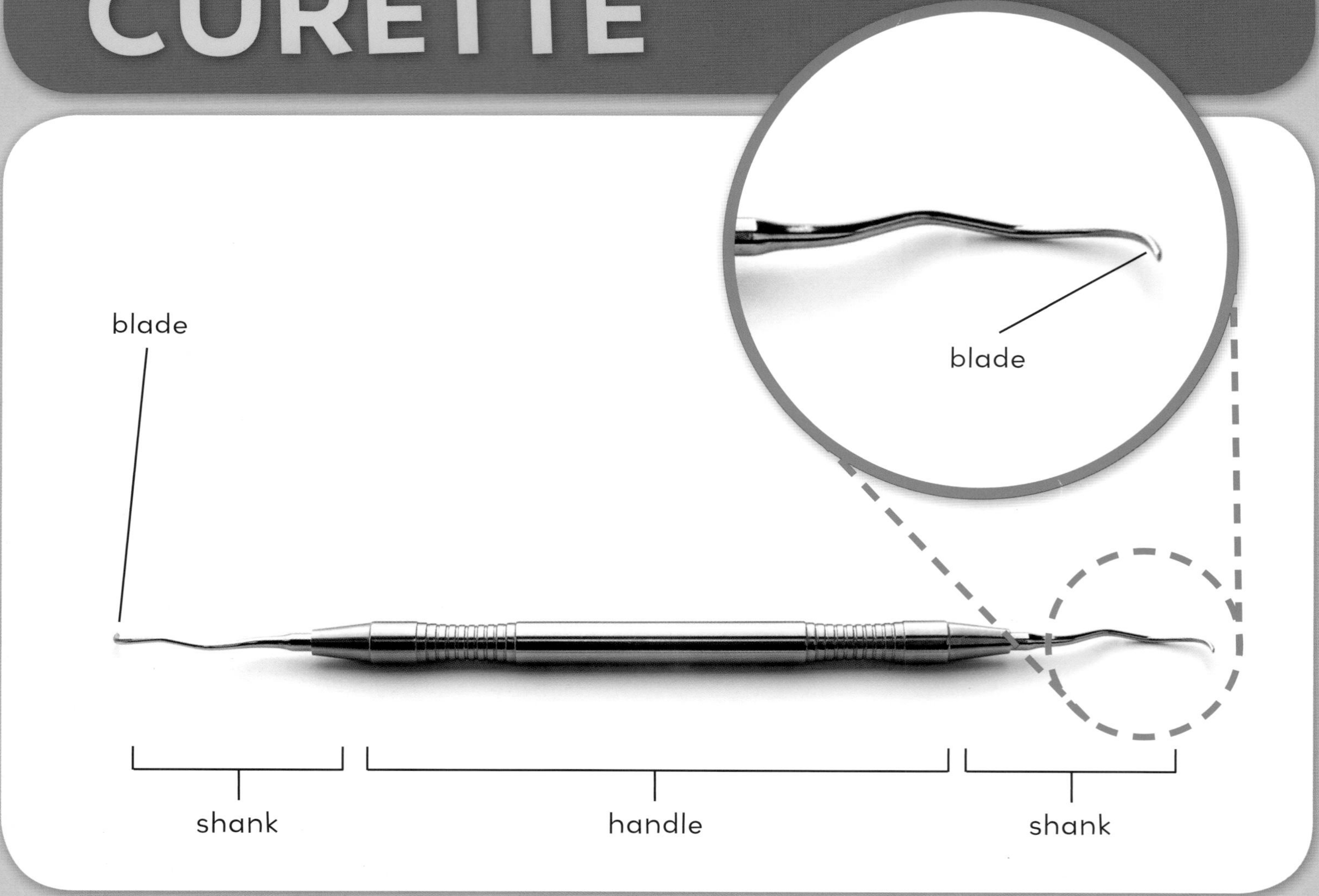

blade

blade

shank

handle

shank

A curette is used to clean the teeth.

Teeth can get covered with **plaque** and tartar. The dentist scrapes the teeth clean with the curette's blades. The dentist often uses a mouth mirror and a curette together.

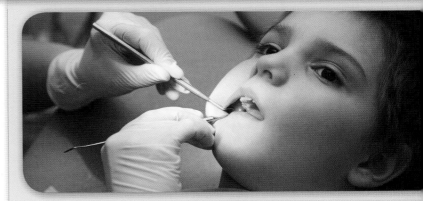

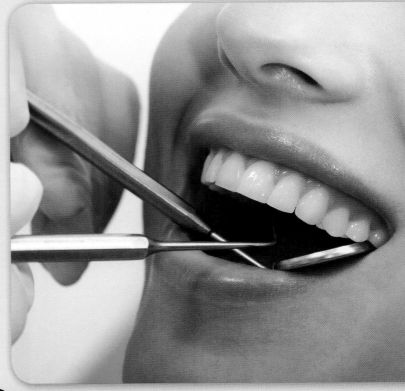

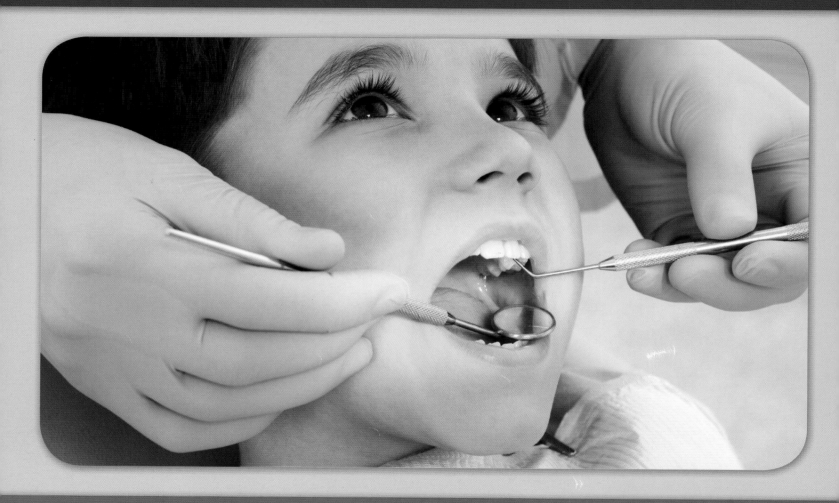

The dentist cleans the backs of Robert's teeth.
She is using a curette and a mouth mirror.

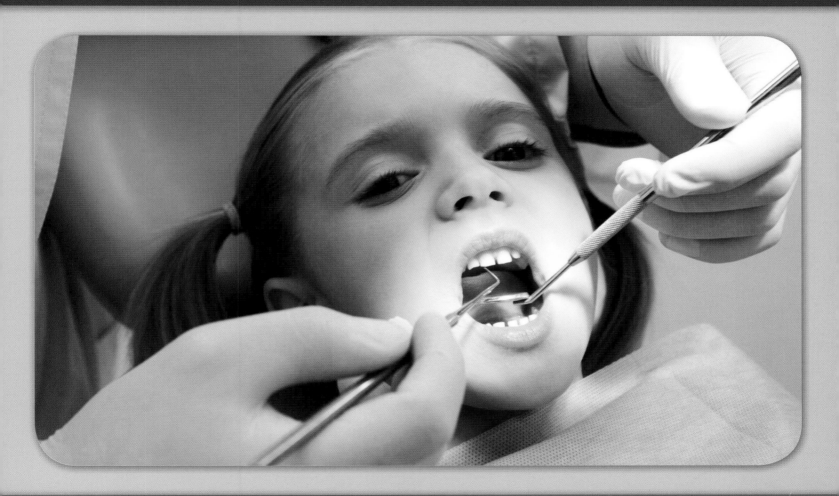

Emily is having her teeth cleaned. The dentist scrapes away plaque and tartar with a curette.

X-RAY MACHINE

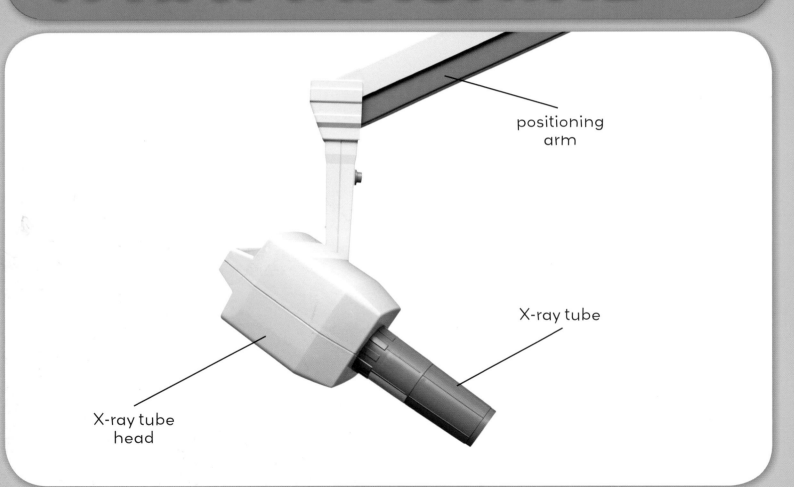

positioning
arm

X-ray tube

X-ray tube
head

An X-ray machine takes pictures of the teeth.

The pictures are called X-rays. The **patient** bites a piece of plastic while the X-rays are taken. The X-rays help dentists find hidden **cavities**.

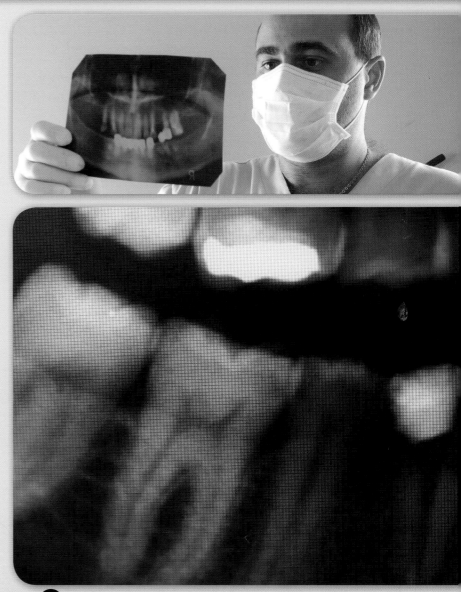

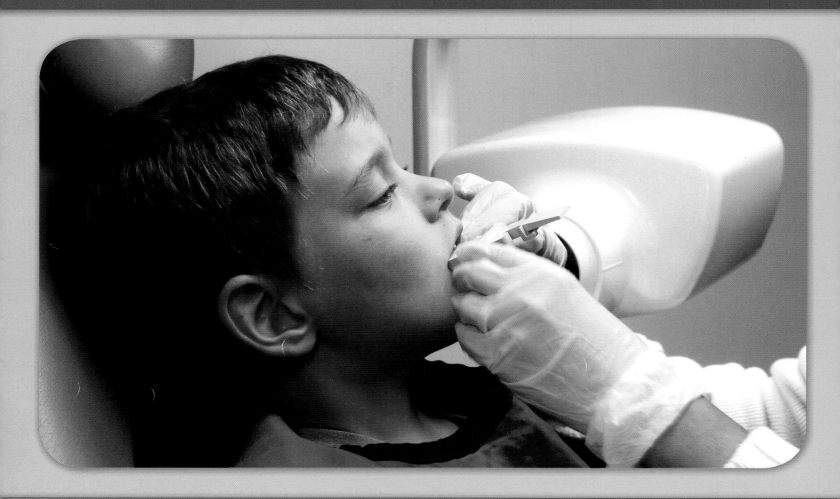

Alex is having his teeth X-rayed. He bites down on a plastic piece. This helps make the X-ray clearer.

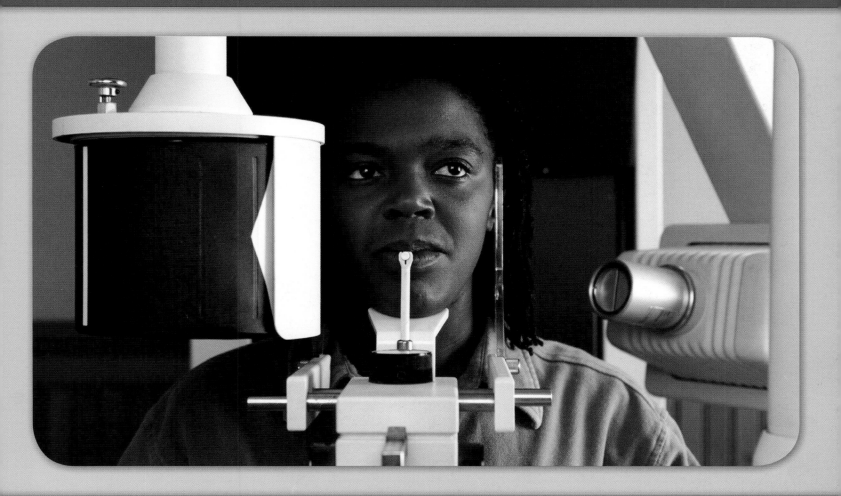

Jaime may have a **cavity**. The dentist will take an X-ray picture to find out for sure.

DENTAL DRILL

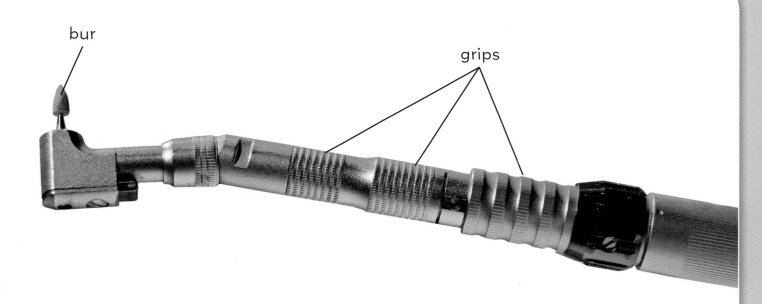

bur

grips

handpiece

A dental drill is used to remove cavities.

The drill's bur spins very fast. The dentist presses the spinning bur against the **cavity**. The bur scrapes the cavity away, leaving a hole in the tooth. Then the dentist fills in the hole.

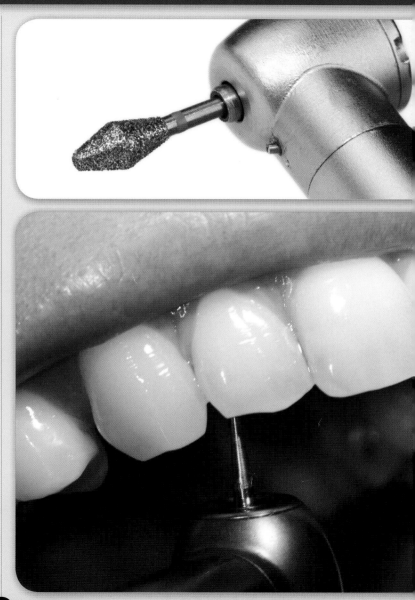

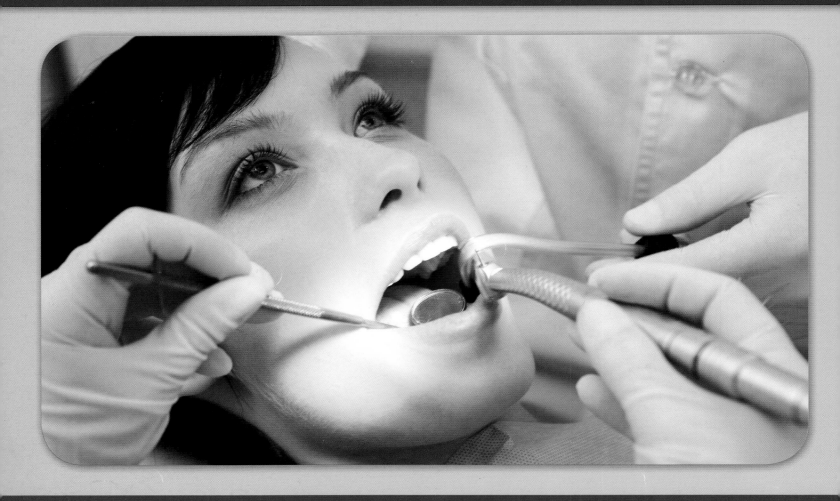

Georgina has a **cavity**. She wants the dentist to remove it before it gets worse.

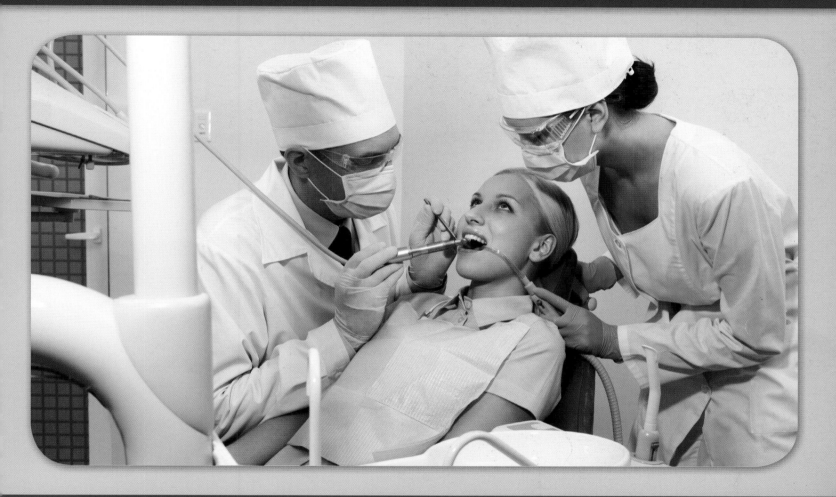

Kara doesn't brush her teeth enough. She has three cavities! The dentist will remove them with a dental drill.

MATCH THE WORDS TO THE PICTURES!

The answers are on the bottom of the page.

MATCH GAME

1. X-ray machine

a.

2. mouth mirror

b.

3. dental drill

c.

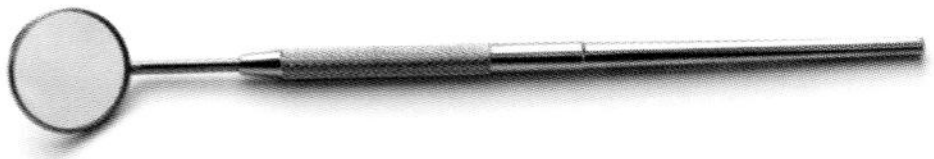

4. curette

d.

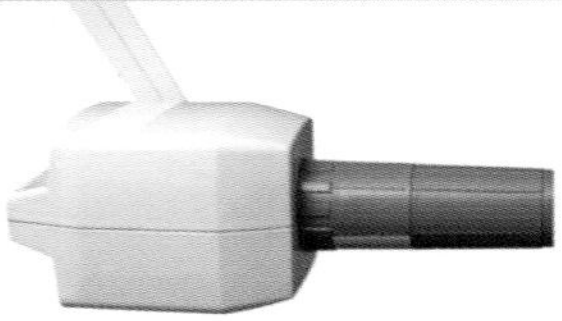

22

TEST YOUR TOOL KNOWLEDGE!

The answers are on the bottom of the page.

1.
Mouth mirrors remove **cavities**.

TRUE OR FALSE?

2.
Curettes scrape away **plaque** and tartar.

TRUE OR FALSE?

3.
X-ray machines take pictures of teeth.

TRUE OR FALSE?

4.
A dental drill is used to see inside the mouth.

TRUE OR FALSE?

TOOL QUIZ

cavity – a spot on a tooth that has started to rot or decay.

checkup – a routine exam by a doctor or dentist.

lead – a kind of metal that is very heavy.

molar – a back tooth with a flat surface for grinding.

patient – a person who receives medical or dental treatment.

plaque – a sticky coating on the teeth that is caused by bacteria in the mouth.

reflect – to cause light, sound, or heat to bounce back.